Contents

Introduction

Welcome to the world of glorious Paintstiks, called both Markal in the U.K. & Europe and Shiva in North America.

Paintstiks are unique as they are created from an oil and wax mixture which gives a smooth slightly greasy medium to work with. Paintstiks should not be confused with other oil bars which require a primed surface and are therefore unsuitable for fabric. This book will try to illustrate numerous different applications, colour combinations and methods of applying paintstiks to fabric and paper.

One of the main features of paintstiks is the generous quantity and variety of pigment colour contained within the cardboard sheath. As soon as this is firmly rubbed across a sheet of paper the rich colour is seen, it attaches to the surface, you can leave it as it is or your can smear or rub it into the paper surface. Paintstiks have to be used, you need to become familiar with their properties, their qualities and the characteristics of the different colours. You must use them for yourself, on to your chosen fabric, paper or surface. With a little experience and practice you will become familiar with the effects you can create.

This book shows and explains some of the many possibilities that I have discovered over many years of using Paintstiks, alone and with a variety of other media.

Paintstiks featured in this book are available in Professional, Iridescent and Metallic colours and are allocated a Series number which reflects the quality and cost of different pigments used in their manufacture. This is reflected in the selling price.

PROFESSIONAL COLOURS
(Standard)

YELLOWS & GREYS

▶ *Azo Yellow* (Series 3) a strong opaque yellow closest to a golden yellow, excellent when mixed with reds to create oranges and gingers. Mix with blues to create soft naturalistic greens.

▶ *Yellow Citron* (Lemon) (Series 3) very acidic opaque yellow, quite green but will give acidity and vibrancy to colour combinations.

▶ *Navy Blue* (Series 2) so dark that it is looks very similar to black, but when mixed with Titanium White creates a blue grey, and when mixed with Azo yellow creates a muted green.

▶ *Paynes Grey* (Series 1) very dark, in fact appearing black but when mixed with white gives quite a warm blue grey as well as creating attractive grey greens when mixed with whites and yellows.

▶ *Ivory Black* (Series 1) a very dense black, showing a slight blueness when mixed with Antique white. Turning to murky green when mixed with Azo yellow.

▶ *Yellow Ochre* (Series 1) a slightly opaque greenish yellow, making colour mixes slightly flat. An excellent colour to mix with blues to give subtle, naturalistic greens.

REDS & PINKS

Dusty Rose (Series 1) a paler version of Mauve, mixing well with Slate and Ice Blue to give warm greys and soft delicate pinks.

Mauve (Series 2) a gingery off pink, not really showing any relationship to violet, purple or lilac but greater similarity to terracotta and light brick reds.

Medium Pink (Series 2) a light pink, very opaque but when mixed with transparent colours such as Azo Yellow, Grape and Antique White can give quite a luminous effect.

Grape (Series 3) the closest colour to magenta, but having a slightly maroon element. A rich colour that will mix with various blues to give purple shades.

Alizarin Crimson (Series 3) a transparent deep red, similar to a rich wine colour. Beautiful when mixed with Iridescent Yellow or Azo Yellow to create rich plum, fruity reds.

Tompte Red (Series 3) rich bright slightly darker red. A strong pigment colour that mixes well with yellows and creates good pinks when mixed with whites.

Napthol Red (Series 3) a deep strong rich red. Mixed with Azo Yellow to produce a range of oranges. Add white to create a range of peaches and pinks.

Azo Orange (Series 3) a strong opaque bright orange, close to Napthol Red, very powerful when applied near other bright opaque colours.

Peach (Series 2) a paler version of Azo Orange, opaque and chalky.

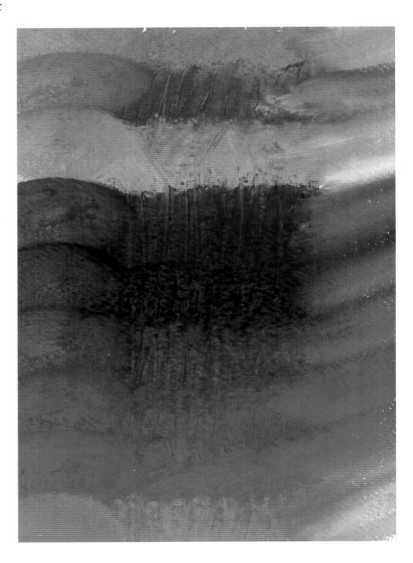

BLUES

▶ *Light Green* (Series 2) a very lively light green, belonging to the turquoise/teal family. A light colour incorporating a substantial quantity of white, this colour gives vibrancy and light opacity to work. Lively colours are obtained when mixed with Lemon Citron or Wedgewood blue.

▶ *Turquoise* (Series 2) strong, rich, slightly turquoise colour. Excellent for using on top of transparent or contrasting colours to give verve and energy to work.

▶ *Teal Blue* (Series 2) the most transparent turquoise colour, very rich in pigment, intense and dark initially but extend with a blender or mix with white to give a wide range of different tones and tints. Teal colour is similar to Turquoise (which is an opaque colour), or Light Green (which has white added) or Iridescent Turquoise that is one of the pearlescent colours.

▶ *Phthalo Blue* (Series 3) a slightly aquamarine blue, very rich in pigment and mixes well with whites to give beautiful tints.

▶ *Prussian Blue* (Series 2) a very dark rich blue, almost a blackish blue, that is very rich in pigment. Mixed with whites it creates slightly greeny blues.

▶ *Ultramarine* (Series 2) a rich strong slightly violet blue, transparent colour, good to mix with Grape to create purples and violets.

▶ *Cobalt Blue* (Series 4) a strong opaque clear blue colour, very vibrant when used in close proximity to Tompte Red, or Azo Orange.

▶ *Purple Sage* (Violet) (Series 2) is similar to Dioxazine purple but is slightly lighter thus giving it an bit of opacity. It is a beautiful rich purple colour, which mixes well with Teal and Ultramarine to create violets and mauves.

▶ *Dioxazine Purple* (Series 4) very strong dark transparent purple, excellent when mixed with Teal and any of the different blues. Blends well with white to give a lilac colour.

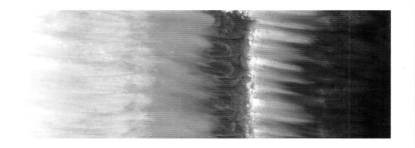

GREENS

‣ *Olive Green* (Series 2) does not appear green when seen in the stick. It is a very deep ochre green, almost the brown of dead leaves. When mixed with white or opaque colours such as mudstone, or slate it becomes a soft neutral colour. Mixed with Teal and Titanium White it is produces a soft greenish grey that will complement many vivid reddish colours.

‣ *Celadon Green* (Series 2) an opaque slightly greyish green colour. When blended with Titanium white it becomes a green /blue grey, useful adjacent to reds and violets.

‣ *Chromium Oxide Green* (Series 4) a very dense naturalistic green rich in pigment, giving a rich flat colour. Mix with yellows to create light leaf greens or with Antique white to make silvery green greys. Add Teal blue and it becomes more transparent and less flat.

‣ *Sap Green* (Series 2) a soft grey green, mix it with Azo Yellow to give a naturalistic green, add white and it becomes a grey green similar to willow leaves.

‣ *Phthalo Green* (Series 3) a rich aquamarine green, very rich in pigment and mixes well to create bright greens with Azo yellow and Yellow Citron. When mixed with whites vibrant greens are achieved similar to distressed metal.

‣ *Viridian* (Series 4) a strong rich transparent green, slightly less blue than Phthalo Green. Excellent when mixed with white to give vibrant aqua colours.

‣ *Meadow Green* (Series 2) a soft slightly opaque naturalistic green.

PALE BLUES & GREYS

▶ *Pewter Grey* (Series 1) a dense black grey, slightly greenish in colour. Mixes well with either whites to give a range of tones.

▶ *Wedgewood Blue* (Series 1) a mysterious gentle blue with a hint of grey. Mix with Ice Blue or Antique White to create classic soft colourings. Mix with Light green, Ice Blue and either white to create watery, icy colours.

▶ *Slate Blue* (Series 2) a rich deep grey blue suggesting stormy skies, windswept seas. Mixes well with whites as well as Pewter Grey and Ice Blue.

▶ *Ice Blue* (Series 2) a surprisingly greenish grey, similar to Celadon

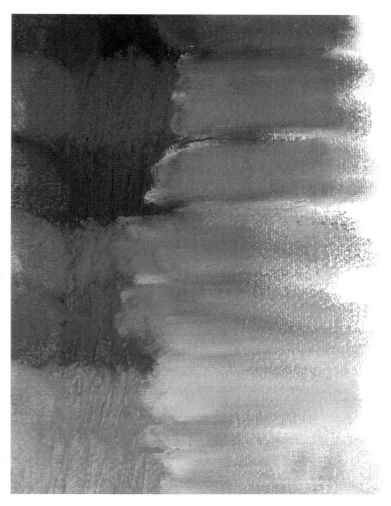

Green with Titanium white. A very useful colour to mix with strong pure colours to lighten or give opacity.

▶ *Mudstone* (Series 2) a really neutral colour, quite calming and a good foil for bright light blues and hot pinks.

▶ *Beige* (Series 2) a slightly pink colour, particularly when placed adjacent to neutral colours such as sandstone and mudstone. Reminiscent of colours found on sandy beaches or in rock pools.

▶ *Sandstone* (Series 2) a slightly chalky, muddy colour – rather like kaolin clay. Attractive when mixed with whites and used adjacent to Ice Blue and Slate.

BROWNS

▶ **Raw Umber** (Series 1) a slightly gingery brown with slight green overtones. Very useful for darkening colours without the addition of black. Add to Teal to create stormy green/blues or mix with Grape to create a rich brown.

▶ **Burnt Umber** (Series 1) a dark transparent blue brown. Needs to be used sparingly when combining with other lighter colours such as yellows.

▶ **Burnt Sienna** (Series 1) a dense rich cedar wood colour, which when thinned with a blender gives a strong red brown. When mixed with Azo yellow, it becomes less transparent but becomes a deep corn colour.

▶ **Asphaltum** (Series 2) a transparent gingery red brown colour, mixes well with Alizarin Crimson.

▶ **Chocolate Brown** (Series 2) a slightly opaque medium brown colour.

▶ **Barn Red** (Series 1) a deep cinnamon colour, fairly opaque, quite a yellowy brown so will give deep petrol colours when mixed with Teal or red earthy colour when mixed with Azo Yellow.

WHITES

▶ **Antique White** (Series 2) slightly creamy white, very opaque. Excellent for blending with Professional colours to create soft tints.

▶ **Titanium White** (Series 2) a pure white, very useful to give opacity or blended with the darker transparent colours such as Phthalo Green or Viridian.

BLENDING STICKS

A Professional Blender (Series 1) is an uncoloured binder stick, useful for extending and thinning Professional colours. The blending stick will make the colour more transparent and will aid the combining of two colours together. It can also be used as a resist, when working with liquid colour such as inks on paper. Generous additions of the blending stick to pure colour on fabric does however tend to stiffen it.

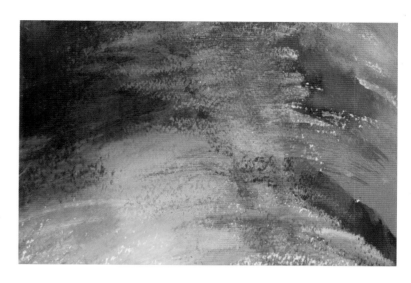

An Iridescent Blending Stick (Series 4) is designed to add pearlescence to professional colours or to extend Iridescent Colours. If used with Professional colours make sure to select the transparent colours such as Grape, Alizarin Crimson, Phthalo Blue and Green to see the full effect of the mixture. The Iridescent Blending stick can also be used to make an Iridescent colour paler, more delicate and ethereal.

Add the Iridescent Blender to a transparent Professional colour such as Teal on paper and blend the two together with your finger, brushing the colour up and down. It will be quite noticeable how the iridescence is lying in the colour mixture when you move the paper in different directions.

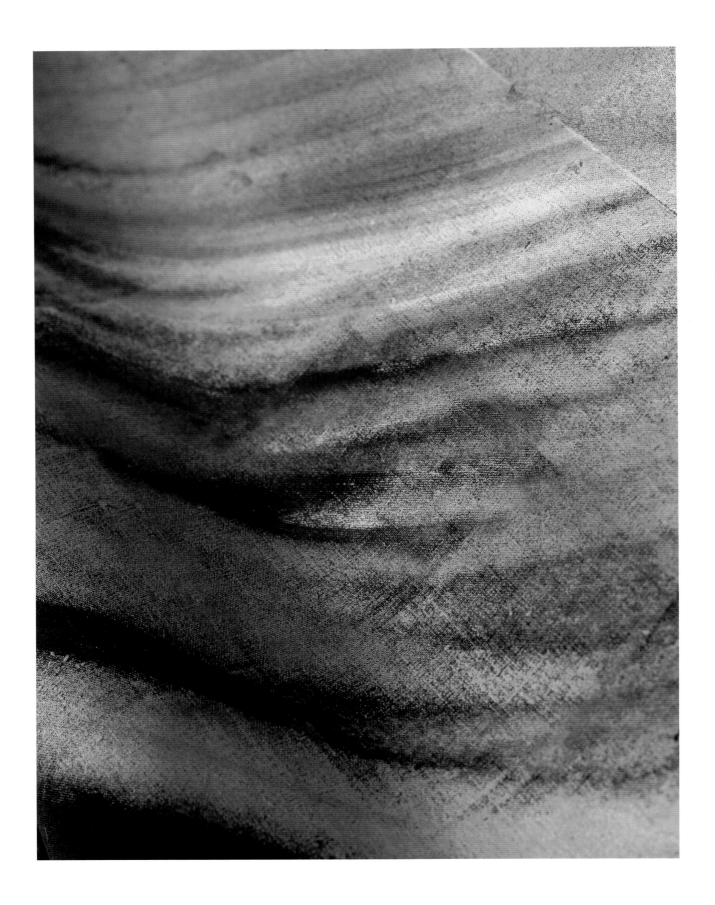

METALLICS

❯ Metallic Gold (Series 4) a really excellent gold colour which contains metal powder thus giving an excellent sheen on all surfaces. Quite soft to apply and needs to be well worked into a fabric to give a good depth of colour.

❯ Metallic Silver (Series 4), a soft rich colour that more resembles pewter than silver.

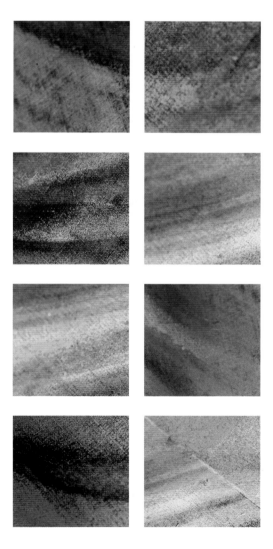

IRIDESCENT COLOURS (all series 4)

Iridescent colours are best applied to a dark surface, where the sheen can be fully appreciated. The addition of an iridescent binder means that the colour has an opacity thus making the colour fully visible. All colours can be mixed together or lightened with the Pearl White. Further subtle variations can be achieved when some of the transparent Professional Markal are mixed with Iridescent colours such as Alizarin Crimson with Iridescent Light Gold to achieve pearlescent burnt orange.

❯ Brown, a deep chocolate brown that works well with Copper and Metallic Gold.

❯ Charcoal, a dark pewter, gunmetal grey.

❯ Copper, a really strong rusty colour that works well with Iridescent Red or makes strong contrasts with Iridescent Turquoise or Blue.

❯ Green, a rich blue-green, rich in pigment and works well with Turquoise and Blue.

❯ Leaf Green, a lovely light golden green that blends well with Light Gold.

◗ Light Gold, an Iridescent yellow ochre that blends well with different blues and greens to expand the colour palette. An excellent colour for adding life to a variety of colour ranges such as reds or browns.

◗ Orange, a light orange that will give delicate shades similar to the inside of shells or crabs shells.

◗ Pearl White, an iridescent white that can be used to lighten darker iridescent colour such as Brown or Charcoal. It can also be used alone to give highlights or tints.

◗ Pink, another pale gentle colour that will blend well with Orange or Turquoise to give delicate almond blossom colours.

◗ Purple, a rich strong colour that blends well with either Turquoise or Blue to give a variety of different mauves and violets. It also works well when placed next to Copper and Iridescent Red.

◗ Red, a strong deep red that is quite similar to Copper. It can be used very effectively adjacent to Purple, Copper and Brown to give rich deep effects.

◗ Blue, a strong electric blue with plenty of punch. Excellent placed next to Turquoise and Green.

◗ Turquoise, a really strong brilliant hue that works very well with a range of different colours. Placed beside greens, Light Gold and blues to give a calming adjacent colour scheme or used as an accent in combination with Copper, Red or Purple.

Accessing The Paintstik Colour

The first thing to remember about a Paintstik is that it has a skin that will need to be removed before applying it to any surface. Either carefully shave this skin off with a craft knife, or firmly rub the stick onto paper to release the skin. Once it is removed the Paintstik will be rich and oily and easy to draw with on paper, plaster, unglazed terracotta, or fabric. Once opened the Paintstiks do have an odour which if used excessively can be quite strong. It is always advisable to work in a well ventilated area. As the Paintstik becomes absorbed into the chosen surface, any odour reduces, especially after the fixing and laundering of fabric.

How To Apply Paintstiks

Direct Application: Getting Started!

On Paper

Use a Paintstik to draw bold strong lines on a firm smooth drawing or cartridge paper.

Feel the colour glide freely from the stick, try a second colour nearby and then blend the two together with your finger.

See how the colours mix, rub it together in circular movements or up and down.

Observe how they blend together, some will be transparent, others opaque, some chalky or even Iridescent.

Try adding the Professional Blending stick to extend the colour, it is very effective with the dark professional colours such as Teal, Phthalo Blue or Dioxazine Purple. The Professional blender will

make colours transparent and oily helping them to mix easily.

Explore the Professional colours such as Medium Pink, which is opaque by adding dark transparent Grape to create rich warm colours.

Add Azo Yellow to Light Green to create vibrant limes and greens.

Paintstiks can be applied onto paper by a variety of direct methods. Extending it with the Professional blender will give a delicate transparent look especially when working it into the paper with your finger.

Alternatively apply it thickly with short strokes, building layers of colour to create a rich textural surface.

On Fabric

Apply Paintstiks directly onto the surface, provided the fabric weave is suitable. Paintstiks can be used on any fibre - natural, man made and synthetic. A firm close woven cotton or canvas will happily absorb a direct Paintstik application, as will a fine tightly woven polyester. However a lightweight fabric such as silk habotai could become clogged and stiff.

Every fabric will have their own characteristics, absorbency and surface finish which need to be taken into consideration when beginning any project.

When directly applying Paintstik, work it well into the fabric surface, making sure it is fully rubbed into the fibres.

For permanency, and laundering, Paintstiks must be heat fixed. It is advisable to leave it to absorb into the surface for at least two days allowing the oiliness to evaporate. If it needs to be laundered, heat fix the Paintstik for four minutes using the hottest temperature setting for the fibre type. Make sure that the fabric has been fully exposed to heat before laundering. If the Paintstik surface seems fresh, oily or greasy, either allow it more time to evaporate or protect your iron before heat setting.

Initially hand wash the fabrics to check it has been fully fixed.

Other Surfaces

Use Paintstiks directly onto unglazed terracotta, wood, plaster and leather by drawing and applying it directly onto the surface making sure the colour is well rubbed in. Allow it to absorb for at least two days.

Methods Of Applying Paintstiks
Direct Application

There are a few guidelines when applying Paintstiks directly.

◗ The first is to use them firmly, pressing hard enough to ensure a rich application. The transparent professional colours often feel softer and oilier than the iridescent colours that are quite firm and will give well defined lines.

◗ The second is to make sure that the colour is well worked into the surface; for fabric by brushing or rubbing; for paper, ceramics or plaster by working the colour into the surface with your finger or a soft cloth.

◗ Thirdly be aware of the visual differences in the Paintstik colours, some are very transparent such as the Professional blues, whereas the yellows have an opacity. The Iridescent colours are also opaque thus being very visible on dark surfaces.

Stencilling

Paintstiks are ideal to use with stencils, they blend easily using a stencil brush or an old toothbrush.

▶ Stencilling on fabric

Select a closely woven fabric, such as medium weight silk such as Duppion or heavier weight calico (muslin).

Tape it firmly to a smooth board or table top.

Place the stencil onto the fabric and apply the Markal gently onto the stencil edge, then brush it into the fabric through the stencil design, taking care not to overload it.

Alternatively rub some colour onto the stencil brush and apply it directly through the stencil onto the fabric.

▶ Stencilling on other surfaces

Prepare the surface by cleaning it and then plan the positioning of the stencils.

Hold the stencil in position, maybe lightly attaching it with masking tape and rub the Paintstik to the stencil surface, then brush the colour through the stencil design.

Carefully lift the stencil away from the surface and check the underside is clean before re-positioning it.

Stencilling gives the opportunity to create subtle colour blends and shading by gently brushing colours together.

It is worthwhile doing a small sample before embarking on your main project.

Applying Paintstiks Using Masks

Paintstiks are easily and effectively applied using a mask. A number of different masking materials are listed below and they can be as complex or as simple as you wish. Using a mask is a convenient and flexible method of applying simple shapes or lines repeatedly to any surface.

A simple torn piece of cartridge paper or masking tape can be used repeatedly down a piece of fabric or paper, giving a strong line when brushed with a strong red or a soft line when brushed with a pale blue.

The most effective method of applying the colour is to work the Paintstik onto the paper mask or tape and brush the colour off onto the surface with a firm toothbrush. This way you can build the density of the colour as well as blending it together with lighter or darker shades to create delightful tonal combinations.

Masks can be created by using a number of different materials.

The following materials will make excellent masks:

Torn masking tape can create random edges to designs.

Cut pieces can give crisp sharp lines, points and precise patterns.

When tearing the tape make sure that the ends are carefully integrated with other shapes or lines. If the masking is not carefully prepared, ugly or abrupt shapes can be created once the Paintstik is applied.

Remember when masking out a design think in reverse and consider the negative spaces.

▶ **Masking Tape** – Available in a number of different permanency and widths. Some lightweight masking tape may move when brushed.

Use masking tape to divide up a fabric, a wall or terracotta pot.

Make an instant unique mask by cutting or tearing the tape.

▶ **Freezer Paper** — a paper that is silicone coated on one side and familiar to patch workers and quilters as a simple heat applied template.

When gently ironed on the matt side, it will temporarily adhere to a fabric. It can be cut or torn, making it very versatile to create complex and intricate designs.

Once the Paintstik has been applied, it is easy to lift the Freezer paper mask and it leaves no residue on the fabric.

▶ **Frisk Film** – a transparent low tack adhesive film that can be used as a temporary mask on paper but also on fabric.

Easily cut with a craft knife thus making it possible to create intricate patterned masks or stencils for use with Paintstiks. Once colouring is complete the film is easily lifted leaving no residue.

▶ **Masking Fluid** – for use on paper. Apply masking fluid or drawing fluid to the areas that you want to protect from the Paintstik colour.

Allow it to dry, then apply the Paintstik. Once it has absorbed into the surface, peel away the masking fluid revealing the original surface.

▶ **Paper masks** – a good quality medium weight drawing paper will provide a very adequate mask for repeated use when applying Paintstiks to a fabric or paper.

A cut or a torn edge can give delicate and individual line when Paintstiks are either rubbed or brushed from it.

Rubbings

Paintstiks are an excellent medium to use for rubbings. Select a smooth absorbent surface which is closely woven. Such fabrics will give fine definition and amazing detail if the Paintstik is sensitively applied. The choice of rubbing surface and the paper or fabric to rub it onto, is key to an exciting and pleasing result.

Textured Surfaces For Rubbings

An enormous range of raised and textured surfaces can be used with Paintstiks.

Any raised surface needs to have an even texture or raised pattern, so that when a rubbing is taken, the Paintstik can make good contact with the pattern under the fabric or paper surface.

Many textures, patterns and everyday objects will make excellent surfaces, just look around any hardware shop, garden centre or toy shop to find different patterns and textures.

▶ **Textured wallpaper** - a large variety of both random textural papers as well as formal geometric patterns can be found. Glue the wallpaper to a firm piece of card to give extra stability and

durability. Look for old rolls of wallpaper designs with unusual patterns to give greater variety.

▶ *Grids and Meshes* – select plastic meshes and grids at garden centres, D.I.Y. centres or model shops. Plastic rug and sewing canvas give interesting checks and regular patterning.

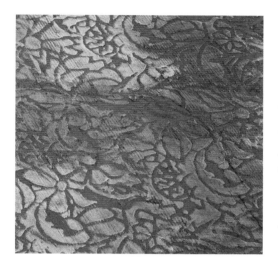

▶ *Print blocks* – your own lino or an up to date equivalent such as PZ Kut print blocks will give excellent rubbings provided the image is crisp. Using lino cutting tools to create individual and intricate patterns, these blocks can create unique effects both on paper and fabric.

▶ *Wooden Indian print blocks* can also be used very effectively.

▶ *Commercial print blocks* are useful as well but sometimes have a handle on the reverse, which can make the block unstable.

▶ *Rubbing Plates* – children's toy shops, hobby and craft shops often sell these plastic double sided textural plates. Often depicting animal markings, simple geometrics such as squares, triangles and linear patterns, these plates can be used repeatedly in different colours giving a quick and exciting pattern.

▶ *Blocks made with unusual textures.*
Select a variety of different heavy weight cotton laces such as curtain lace or crocheted towel edging. Glue the lace to a firm piece of card or board, keeping the surface as even as possible.

▶ *Drawn Individual patterns* – use thick glue pens, glue guns or a 3D pen to draw a pattern, words or images onto a firm card. Allow to dry, then place it under the surface of the cloth to take a rubbing.

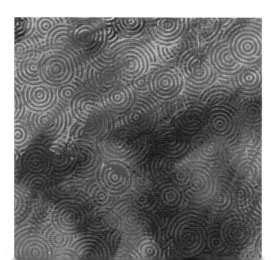

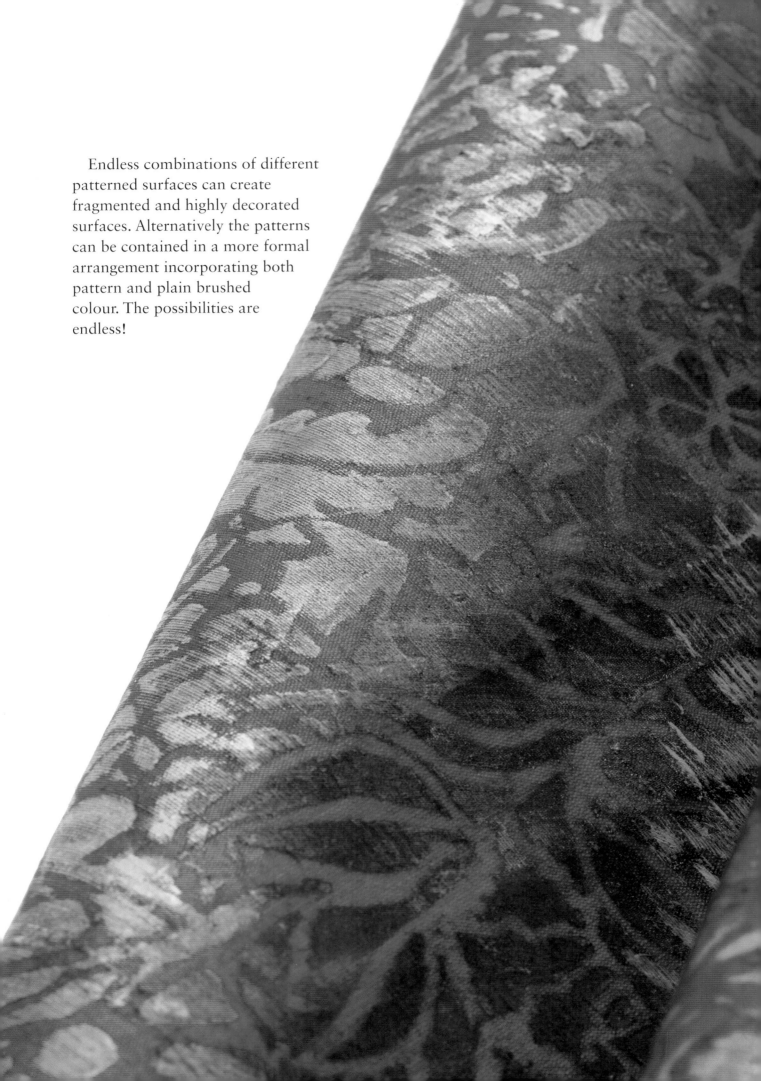

Endless combinations of different patterned surfaces can create fragmented and highly decorated surfaces. Alternatively the patterns can be contained in a more formal arrangement incorporating both pattern and plain brushed colour. The possibilities are endless!

Paintstiks And Paper

Professional and Iridescent Paintstiks provide a rich easily applied medium for a wide variety of paper types. Despite being rather chunky they encourage strong bold applications and the richness of the colour soon gives visual rewards.

Whether using Paintstiks as a drawing tool or to create a purely decorative effect it is worth choosing a good quality paper to work on. Select a heavier weight drawing paper, cartridge or even a Khadi cotton rag paper that has a good sized finish and will allow the colour to be applied to the paper surface.

Remember that the Paintstik is made from oil and wax and will work easily into the paper surface. Smear and blend the rich colours together with your fingers and work it into the paper surface.

Using pure Professional colours with Iridescent colours on white and neutral papers can work well giving unusual colour combinations as well as surface variations. Iridescent colours are very effective on dark papers including heavy weight brown paper.

Using Paintstiks on paper is not for the faint hearted, they ask to be used with generous strokes and can be easily extended with a professional blending stick or given added pearlescence using an iridescent blending stick.

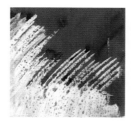

Paintstiks blended and rubbed with the fingers can build an excellent patina to a paper surface.

A dark highly textured paper can be cherished and enhanced by repeated applications of Iridescent colours to build rich waxy finishes which make them ideally suitable for book covers or inclusion in paper collage.

Meanwhile strong primary Professional colours can be drawn onto crisp white paper to give dynamic and bold imagery.

The Paintstik quickly absorbs into the paper surface but if applied thickly can take a few days to fully dry.

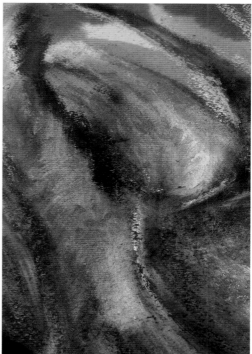

Paintstiks As A Resist

As Paintstiks are made of oil and wax they are a very good resist on paper for all water based products.

A simple application of the Professional Blending Stick will provide a resist on watercolour paper when using watercolours or inks.

Layers of colour can be applied, allowed to dry and then further applications of the Blending Stick can be used to build up a strata of colour.

Consider using layers of ink, then allowing them to dry before masking areas with the Professional Blender. Then apply a further layer of dark sepia or black ink to highlight the protected areas.

Use the Paintstik Professional colours onto white paper, building and blending colours together working in bands, strips or areas. Then apply a wash of darker coloured ink across the Paintstik while fresh. Watch the Paintstik resist the inks, blot away excess ink if desired or leave it to dry on the surface.

Every experiment will be different, but the combination of ink and Paintstik is free flowing, exciting and unique.

Even Paintstiks that have been applied some months previously can still form some type of resist. Printing onto Paintstik using acrylic can create unexpected effects especially when an ink is applied once the acrylic has dried.

Paintstiks With Inks

A very cheap and colourful ink can be created with Procion MX dye. This is a cold water dye for natural fibres that is also an excellent ink on paper.

Ink recipe:

¼ - ½ a teaspoon of dye powder dissolved in 100mls of hot water makes a strong coloured ink. Store in clearly labelled jars in a secure place away from children and vulnerable adults.

(Procion MX Dye must be treated with care, always mix in a designated dyeing area, wear a mask when mixing and dissolving the dye powder and wear rubber gloves and protective clothing when preparing and using it.)

Paintstiks and inks on paper will give quick, exciting and dynamic results. Used boldy and bravely the reaction of the fluid inked colour against and over the Paintstik can be electric.

Paintstiks and Ink on white paper

Use a strong white paper that will take the oily Paintstik colour without lifting the surface and will absorb the liquid colour happily. Begin by applying the Paintstik colour in strong firm lines blending colours together with your fingers. Leave areas of the white paper uncoloured and then apply washes of ink across the paper covering both the Paintstik and the plain paper. Let the ink dry, observe how the liquid colour absorbs into the paper changing colour as it dries and how it can form little beads of colour on the surface of the Paintstik. As it dries, if you wish to blot the paper take a similar sheet of paper or a lighter weight and press it onto the Paintstik and inked areas.

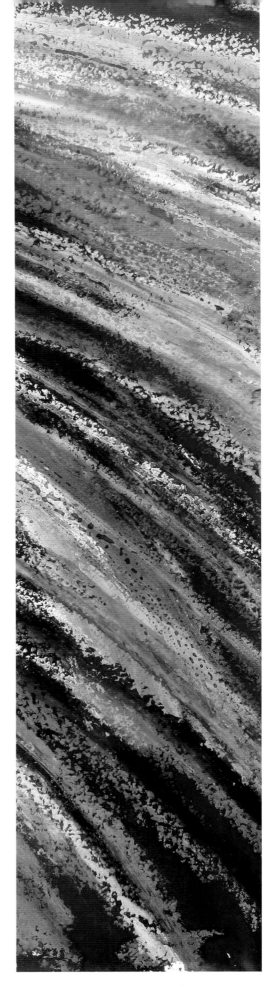

Repeat the process as you feel necessary or even scratch back into the Paintstik to distress the surface and then re-ink.

Paintstik and Ink on darker papers

Select a medium to dark paper, such as green, blue or purple and draw with a selection of Iridescent Paintstik colours. Apply the Paintstik thickly and then push the colour up and down with your fingers. Hold the paper to the light and see how the Iridescent mica flakes within the stick reflect the light and give a dimensional surface to the Paintstik. Apply a darker ink across the Paintstik and onto the background paper altering the colour and making it darker in some areas.

Once this paper is dry it can be used for collage or cut and manipulated, folded or torn giving wonderful iridescent sheens to pieces of work.

Ruched inked paper surfaces and Paintstiks

By gluing tissue paper to a backing sheet, unusual surfaces can be achieved. Carefully apply ink onto the ruched surface letting the colours mix and bleed into each other. Leave the paper to dry completely. Select an opaque Paintstik of a contrasting colour and gently rub it across the raised, manipulated surface to create a unique paper.

Paintstiks and Acrylics

One of the most unexpected qualities of Paintstiks are that they can be used to make subtle colour changes to acrylic colour. Use coloured acrylic for printing, painting or with acrylic gels to give dimensional surfaces, then adjust the colour by rubbing contrasting Paintstik colours onto the dried acrylic. It can enhance the colour very gently, slightly making a yellow more orange with the addition of Napthol Red or add an iridescent sheen to a dark grey by the addition of an Iridescent Violet.

Occasionally when working with acrylic gels, the surface of the acrylic has a delicate pattern that can be enhanced with a light application of a contrasting Paintstik colour such as Turquoise or Ice Blue.

Paintstiks can also be used in combination with acrylic printing, block, mono printing or roller printing. It can be blended into the acrylic and the paper background before it is inked to give extra variety and depth.

Using Paintstiks on a Large Scale

Finally in this section of exploring Paintstiks with paper, why not be really brave and try using them on a larger scale. Take a large sheet of paper and if possible tape it to an upright surface such as a board or a firm wall. Put some newspaper down to protect the floor and start drawing using the Paintstik in big broad generous sweeps. Use your whole body, holding the Paintstik firmly and allowing it to make generous sweeping marks across the paper. Professional Paintstik colours are particularly good as

they are slightly soft and the colour will flow easily. Lay different colours adjacent to each other and blend or rub them together to give subtle variations.

If you need the colour to move more easily add some Blending Stick to help the colour to become more oily.

Try drawing enormous plants or flowers or even figures using the Paintstik colour, you may well be amazed what you can achieve!

Further Thoughts For Paintstiks On Fabric

Paintstiks On Dark Fabrics

When using Paintstiks on a dark fabric such as black, dark brown or navy blue it is important to be aware if the Paintstik colour is transparent, semi opaque, opaque or iridescent. All transparent colours will alter when worked onto a dark fabric and the colour will be almost invisible. This can be rectified by the addition of an opaque white, but the colour will have changed. Another alternative is to use an iridescent equivalent on the fabric and the colour will be vibrant and visible. Some of the opaque and semi opaque colours will also become visible on darker fabrics such as Azo Yellow, Wedgwood Blue or Turquoise.

Remember that Metallic Gold and Silver contain metallic powders so that they will give a very visible appearance.

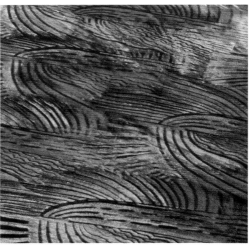

Paintstiks On Light Fabrics

The selection of Professional colours for use on light coloured fabrics must be taken with care. Some darker colours such as Dioxazine Purple, Phthalo Green and Prussian Blue appear very dark. They are rich in dark pigment colour and probably need to be combined with a more opaque colour such as Wedgwood Blue or Slate Grey, to give a degree of opacity on a very light fabric.

The selection of colours is also dependant on the type of application being used. It is less easy to blend colours when undertaking an intricate rubbing, whereas brushing colour from a mask gives plenty of opportunity to create a wide variety of different subtle blends.

Paintstiks And Prints

Both Professional and Iridescent Paintstiks offer a number of different applications when used with previously printed fabrics.

Consider some of the following options:

❯ Use Paintstiks to alter the background colour of a commercially printed fabric by brushing transparent Professional colour onto the fabric. The Paintstik colour will absorb into the unprinted surface, thus altering the background colour. It may also alter the print colour giving unexpected and subtle effects.

❯ When printing onto a shiny fabric such as a satin, try brushing some Professional colour onto the surface, it will often turn slightly matt giving a contrasting surface as well as a change of colour. This can be very effective as contrast to a pearlescent print.

❯ Use Paintstiks to give additional emphasis to a printed pattern or to highlight a specific area of decoration. Rub toothbrush bristles across the Paintstik and then blend it around the area of decoration to be enhanced.

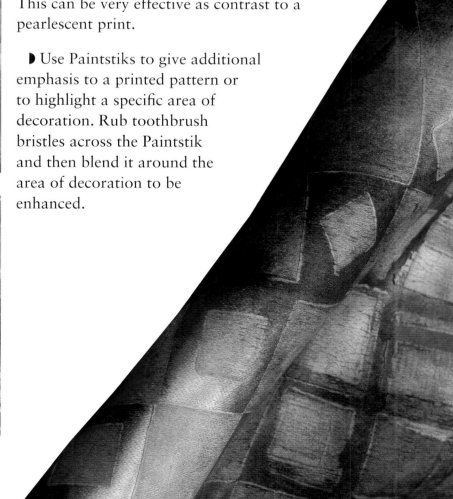

Paintstiks Over A Dyed Or Coloured Surface

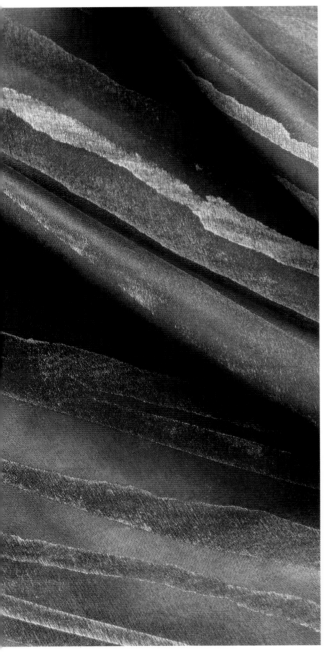

Professional Paintstik colours are particularly useful for giving additional subtle colour adjustments to a flat dyed or coloured fabric. Adjacent colours can be subtly brushed onto the surface giving variety to the original colour. For instance a pale blue fabric could be altered by the addition of Light Green and Ice Blue or made darker by applications of Ultramarine, Turquoise and Teal. Meanwhile a red fabric could be made more vibrant and flame like with additions of Azo Orange and Azo Yellow to give sharp accents of brilliant colour.

Even fabric that has been dyed with tie dye, low immersion or space dye techniques can have further subtle enhancements by the addition of transparent Professional colours which might help to blend rather disparate colour schemes together.

Paintstiks And Dyeing Afterwards On Fabric

When the Paintstik has been applied onto a white or neutral ground, you may wish to give additional colour to the surface. If possible allow the Paintstik to fully absorb into the fabric and even heat fix it before adding additional dye colour. Try some of the following possibilities:

▶ Try bucket dyeing a white fabric that has been brushed with some opaque Professional colours. As there is no Fuchsia or Magenta coloured Paintstiks, try colouring a piece with yellows, whites and ice green Paintstiks and then immerse it in a bright pink dye bath. See how the dye will surround the Paintstik and how the colours will vary in tone depending on the density of application to give a unique fabric.

▶ Divide up your uncoloured fabric into regular squares or triangles and use blended Paintstik colours to create a grid. Once fixed and dry, paint cold water dye directly onto the fabric observing how the dye will impregnate the surface of the fabric sometimes running behind the Paintstik or even being resisted by it where it is densely applied. The results can be mouth watering as you can adjust the colour as you paint but the image you have applied with the Paintstik will remain crisp and clear.

▶ Using dye with Paintstiks can also give the option of introducing truly transparent colour which will fully absorb into the fabric surface which can look stunning in contrast with bold Paintstik colour and shapes.

▶ Remembering that Paintstiks can be applied to all types of fabric means that once it is fixed it can be over coloured using synthetic dyes such as Transfer colour or Disperse dyes, which introduces another possibility for those who like to use synthetic fabric.

Paintstiks Added To Quilted And Stitched Surfaces

Soft rich Paintstik colours such as Titanium White, Turquoise or Yellow Citron can easily be drawn directly on a soft fabric surface. This allows you to add extra colour or detailing after a fabric has been stitched or quilted.

▶ Having quilted a fabric, gently rub a soft Paintstik colour across the surface, taking care to ensure the colour has been absorbed into the fabric. It is well worth cutting the end of the stick before you start so that the colour is soft and clean and adheres easily to the quilted surface. If it is necessary to wash the fabric afterwards make sure the Paintstik is set by addition of heat to the surface for 4 minutes.

▶ For purely decorative effects Paintstiks can be rubbed over and into densely stitched surfaces as well as interesting textural surfaces such as old lace. Try rich Iridescent colours by adding Gold, Copper and Brown to give extra excitement to a dark surface such as black, petrol blue or olive green.

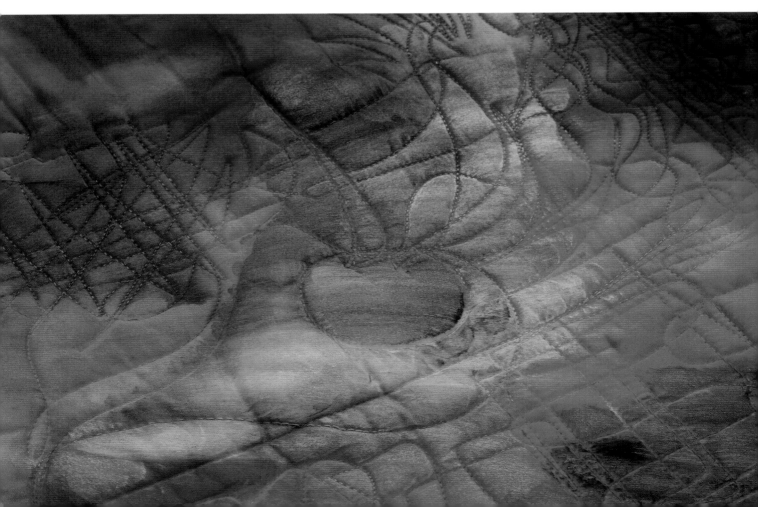

Fabric Ideas

Applying Paintstiks By Brushing And Blending From Masks

Shaded Squares

Once you have mastered the basic technique of applying Paintstiks to different fabrics, you will be ready to really explore the full potential of the wonderful colour palette.

The following process is fairly simple, leaving you ample opportunity to discover colour combinations and mixtures.

❯ Select a close woven white or cream fabric such as calico (muslin) or cotton poplin.

❯ Iron it and attach it firmly to a flat board or table top with masking tape.

❯ Divide the fabric into 8 -10 cm squares using the masking tape.

❯ Select a group of Professional Paintstik colours that will blend and mix well together to give beautifully graduated colours or vibrant contrasts.

Suggestions For Colour Combinations

TRY – Wedgewood Blue, Light Green, Yellow Citron and Purple Sage

TRY – Azo Orange, Azo Yellow, Napthol Red worked together with a contrast of Phthalo Blue and Titanium White

TRY - Sage Green, Slate Blue, Antique White and Ice Blue

TRY- Dioxazine Purple, Cobalt Blue, Napthol Red and Yellow Ochre for a bright combination

TRY –Turquoise, Mudstone, Yellow Citron, Tompte Red and Viridian

TRY – Phthalo Green, Phthalo Blue, Titanium White, Azo Yellow

TRY – Medium Pink, Grape, Azo Yellow and Antique White

You may notice that many of these colours are opaque. This will give a wonderful chalky quality to the colour when applied to the fabric especially when the colours are blended together.

Some are deep rich transparent colours such as Phthalo Blue or Green and Dioxazine Purple, so try blending them with the lighter whites, Mudstone or opaque blues like Wedgewood.

◗ Make sure that you have a clean toothbrush for each colour and begin by rubbing a colour on one side of a square. Brush this colour away from the masking tape onto the fabric.

◗ Take a second colour and rub it onto the masking tape on the next side of the square.

◗ By brushing the colour away from you, begin to work the colour onto the fabric blending and mixing the colours as you work with your brush.

◗ Make sure that you really work the colour densely into the surface of the fabric and keep working the colours together until you are happy with the mixed colour effect.

◗ As you work across the fabric begin to alter the colour combinations and do not be afraid to put further masks across the square to introduce additional colours.

◗ Enjoy the colour mixtures, there are so many combinations that work beautifully together and you will soon become familiar with them. If you feel unsure of how a colour will look try out the colours on a separate piece of paper before you start. (This is always useful as a reference book for the future) There is plenty of information about the characteristics of the colours in the opening section of this book.

◗ Once you are satisfied with the finished work, carefully remove the masking tape, even store that in your sketchbook as inspiration, and allow the Paintstik to absorb into the fabric for a couple of days.

◗ Remember to heat fix the fabric before laundering.

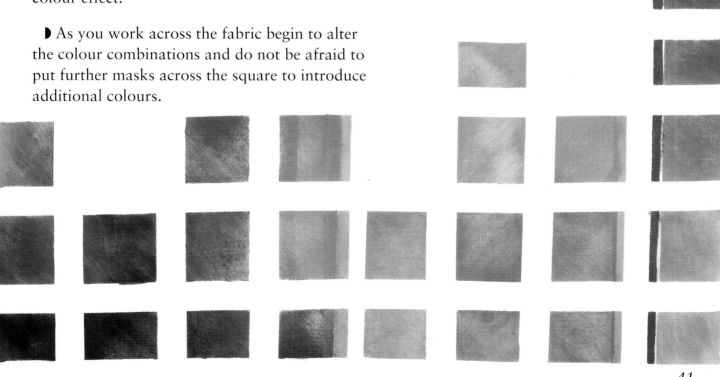

Combining Patterns And Areas Of Colour

Once you have become familiar with using your Paintstiks, by exploring the different colours and the effects that they create, it is important to take them much further. With a bit of forethought and planning, different layers of Paintstiks can be applied to fabric so that both the background can be coloured with flat colour and further Paintstik patterns applied on the surface.

Coloured and Patterned Paintstik Fabric.

▶ Select a dark smooth fabric and tape it to a board.

▶ Divide up the fabric into different sections, squares, triangles or rectangles with carefully cut masking tape.

▶ Using a limited selection of Iridescent colours, such as Copper, Red and Brown colour the fabric by brushing the colours evenly from the masking tape across the defined areas.

▶ Leaving the masking tape in position allow the Paintstik to absorb into the fabric over night.

▶ Select a well defined patterned surface, maybe your own print block or a rubbing block.

▶ Slide the block under the fabric surface by removing the tape from one side and evenly apply a contrasting Iridescent colour such as Turquoise, Blue or Purple by rubbing the surface.

▶ Using the colours in combination gives plenty of opportunity to create uniquely coloured and textured designs.

▶ Once the Paintstik has all been applied, remove the masks and evaluate the result.

If you wish to add extra colour highlights or contrasts, re-tape the specific area and apply the colour.

Once you are satisfied with the finished piece allow to rest for at least 48 hours for the Paintstiks to absorb into the fabric and the oil to evaporate. Then heat fix for permanency.

Natural Colour – Natural Forms

Using Torn Masking Tape To Create A Design On Fabric

❱ Select a light coloured closely woven fabric such as cotton calico (muslin).

❱ Attach the ironed fabric to a smooth board or table top using masking tape.

❱ Select Paintstik colours – for instance Burnt Sienna, Burnt Umber, Alizarin Crimson, Asphaltum, Barn Red, Yellow Ochre, Teal and Titanium White. Make sure you have a toothbrush for each colour.

❱ Prepare the fabric for application of the Paintstiks by taping it in horizontal torn strips. Make sure that all the edges are torn to give a random and naturalistic look.

❱ Beginning in the middle of the fabric, rub Burnt Sienna onto the masking tape adding some Yellow Ochre to vary the colour.

❱ With a thick layer of Paintstik on the tape take a toothbrush and work the Paintstik firmly into the fabric, lifting it from the tape onto the fabric. Always brush away from yourself to prevent the masking tape catching on the brush.

❱ Continue to brush the colour from the mask until you have used all the colour on the tape and the fabric has distinctly changed colour. Make sure the colour has fully impregnated the fabric.

❯ Repeat the process with all the lines of masking tape, gradually working towards you, varying and blending the colours. Try the following combinations: Barn Red and Alizarin Crimson, Burnt Umber and Yellow Ochre, Asphaltum and Titanium White.

❯ Turn the board through 180 degrees and repeat the process working the opposite side of the masks until you have completely coloured all the areas between the masking tape.

❯ Carefully remove one area of masking tape and replace it slightly over the area that has been recently worked. Press into position and add further Paintstiks maybe slightly altering the colour.

❯ Repeat this process of mixing the colours and varying the position of the masking tape.

❯ Finally place two torn edges of masking tape close together, press down firmly and then directly apply a contrasting colour, for instance Teal and Titanium White combined. Work the colour into the fabric gently using your finger to give a smooth blended colour.

❯ By moving the masking tape shapes across the fabric the design will have a rhythm and a cohesive quality.

❯ You may find that the surface of the masking tape becomes discoloured with Paintstik, so that subsequent colours become unattractive or mixed. Either allow the tape to dry over night or lightly clean the surface of the tape with a baby wipe.

❯ Once the application of Paintstik is complete, leave it to absorb into the fabric for 48 hours and then heat set.

The incredible thing about Paintstiks is despite having used them on paper and fabric for years, suddenly a new application comes to mind and the excitement is there all over again. What if I try this colour with this paper, or this combination with that fabric used in a different method? New ideas are always occurring. Recently I have been rubbing the Paintstik thickly onto a paper surface then turning it over and placing it on a print and scratching into the reverse to get a transferred impression of the Paintstik in a specific position.

I continually use them in my sketchbooks; they are wonderful for creating free vibrant background surfaces, that give energy and freedom to a piece of work.

Paintstiks can be combined together to give the most sizzling and rich fabrics especially when combined with electric dye colours painted directly onto a fabric. Bright and joyous, sizzling and acidic, all ready to be enjoyed in itself or as part of further work.

Use this book as a starting point, explore the sheer variety on offer, explore the differing characteristics of the colours and most of all do not be fearful of having a go and making your own piece of work.

Acknowledgements

All illustrations in this publication are from original pieces of work by Ruth Issett.

She would like to thank Viv Arthur, Kevin Mead, Gill Collinson and Chas Issett for their help, skill and expertise in the writing and production of this book.

Ruth Issett lives in Shropshire where she works on her varied textiles and art pieces. Her passion for colour is central to her work but she also enjoys sharing her experience and skills through her teaching worldwide.

She is often associated with Art Van Go with whom she has collaborated, especially at the large textile shows where she is often seen demonstrating different processes and materials especially Paintstiks.

ISBN 0-9554048-3-5

9 780955 404832

www.artvango.co.uk

£9.95

MÉTODO DE ESPAÑOL PARA EXTRANJEROS

PRISMA
CONSOLIDA

comienza

continúa

progresa

avanza

consolida

perfecciona

NIVEL C1

Edi numen

Equipo prisma